D1252561

INHALANTS

Some teens turn to drugs when they feel unhappy, lonely, or isolated.

INHALANTS

Clifford Sherry

THE ROSEN PUBLISHING GROUP, INC.
NEW YORK

The people pictured in this book are only models; they in no way, practice or endorse the activities illustrated. Captions serve only to explain the subjects of the photographs and do not imply a connection between the real-life models and the staged situations shown. News agency photographs are exceptions.

Published in 1994 by The Rosen Publishing Group, Inc.
29 East 21st Street, New York, NY 10010

Copyright 1994 by The Rosen Publishing Group, Inc.

First Edition

Library of Congress Cataloging-in-Publication Data

Sherry, Clifford J.
    Inhalants / Clifford Sherry. — 1st ed.
      p. cm. — (The Drug abuse prevention library)
    Includes bibliographical references and index.
    ISBN 0-8239-1704-5
    1. Solvent abuse—United States—Juvenile literature.
    2. Solvent abuse—Juvenile literature. [1. Solvent abuse.
    2. Substance abuse.] I. Title. II. Series.
    HV5822.S65S44 1994
    362.29′9—dc20   94-572
                                              CIP
                                              AC

Manufactured in the United States of America

Contents

Introduction

*I*n the early 1960s, it became clear that people, especially young people, were sniffing or huffing model airplane glue. Sniffing entails squeezing a tube of glue into a paper or plastic bag, placing the bag over the nose and mouth and inhaling through the nose. The huffer inhales through the mouth.

Within a short time, the sniffer (or huffer) feels woozy, and probably a bit giddy as well. In other words, drunk! He or she will be uncoordinated (unable to walk in a straight line), and have slurred speech. The effect lasts from a few minutes to a few hours.

How Does It Work?

Model airplane glue contains solvents. People have been using and abusing alcohol for centuries, but scientists still do not fully understand how alcohol makes people drunk. The use of solvents for getting high is much more recent. Scientists do not understand how solvents make people drunk.

What Is a Solvent?

A solvent is a substance, usually a liquid, in which things dissolve.

Water is a solvent. The chemical composition of water is H_2O. That means two parts hydrogen to one part oxygen. Hydrogen and oxygen are gases.

Sugar, salt, and baking soda are examples of chemicals that dissolve in water. Each food we eat is composed of complex chemicals. These chemicals give our foods their unique flavors. Caffeine is the chemical in coffee that acts as a stimulant. Coffee, tea, and soup are made up of dozens of chemicals, which are dissolved in the water we cook with.

Many solvents used commercially are chemicals in liquid form. These solvents dissolve other chemicals.

Water is a useful solvent for many

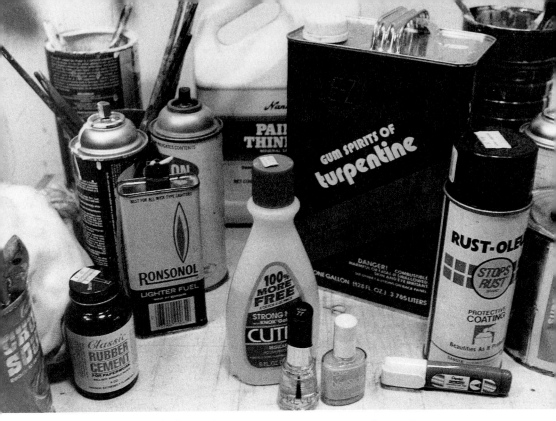

Inhaling solvents can cause permanent brain damage.

purposes. One characteristic of water is that it evaporates slowly. Another characteristic is that some chemicals, like fats (the scientific name is lipids), will not dissolve in it.

Alcohol is also a solvent. There are many kinds of alcohol, and some of them are poisonous. Alcohol evaporates more rapidly than water. Some chemicals that will not dissolve in water will dissolve in alcohol. Wine, beer, and whiskey are mixtures of water and alcohol. This alcohol is produced from the fermentation of the wine grapes or the grains used in whiskey.

Wine is composed of dozens of different chemicals, which give wine its flavor and aroma.

But for some commercial uses alcohol is considered too expensive. It may also be unsuitable because there are some chemicals that will not dissolve in it. So scientists have searched and continue to search for other solvents.

Other Solvents
Benzene is another solvent with many uses. It was isolated from coal tar in 1825.

Scientists have continued to develop solvents for industrial and medical use. Today there are thousands. The ones discussed here are called industrial, or commercial, chemicals.

Most solvents are made from coal or coal tar, oil, or natural gas. Each commercial solvent has different properties and uses.

Solvents are found in a wide variety of products that we use every day. Paint, adhesives, nail polish, and typewriter correction fluid all contain solvents. For example, the solvents in paint carry tiny particles of color or dyes.

Some solvents are sold in their pure,

10 or original, form without anything suspended in them. Dry cleaning fluids are solvents. So are gasoline, lighter fluid, nail polish remover, paint remover, and paint thinner.

Some products carry a high proportion of solvents. For example, about 25% of the weight of model airplane glue is the solvent toluene. Depending on the brand, airplane glue may also contain a variety of other solvents. These include acetone, hexane, and ethyl acetate. For example, the acetone content can be as high as 30 to 85 per cent. Airplane glue may also contain naphtha, isopropanol, or ethanol.

The solvents in model airplane glue have nitrocellulose, cellulose acetate, or polystyrene dissolved in them. These solvents evaporate at room temperature. When they evaporate they leave the glue behind. The substance that makes the glue stick is, itself, a complex chemical.

Products containing solvents are available to everyone. Their misuse is difficult, if not impossible, to control. Solvents or products containing solvents are available in supermarkets and department stores. They are also available in drugstores, hardware stores, and hobby shops.

Health Problems Caused by Solvents

Solvents can cause serious health problems, including permanent brain damage. That is why the amount of solvents that people are exposed to should be carefully controlled. Many people are exposed to dangerous levels of solvents without realizing it. This applies to people using chemicals at home, as well as at work.

Most labels carry warnings about using products in poorly ventilated areas.

There are laws intended to protect people in the workplace, but they are seldom obeyed. Sometimes the employer is at fault. Sometimes the workers themselves ignore safety rules.

The concentration of solvents is expressed in parts per million (ppm). Most people have trouble visualizing 1 ppm.

A typical bedroom is about 10 feet long by 10 feet wide by 8 feet high. It would take about 5 teaspoons of solvent to cause concentration of 1 ppm of the air in the bedroom.

The maximum allowable concentration of toluene for workers is 200 ppm. Sniffers who put airplane glue in paper bags and who put these bags over their noses and mouths to inhale may be exposed to fifty times that amount. That is 10,000 ppm!

Using drugs only makes your problems worse.

CHAPTER 1

What Do Solvents Do?

"Getting high" is how people describe the abuse of solvents. "Getting low" would be a better description. Solvents are depressants. They decrease the activity of the nervous system.

Headache, lightheadedness, drowsiness, and dizziness are symptoms of central nervous system depression. Like alcohol, solvents cause slurred speech.

Depressants cause a decrease in social and sexual inhibitions in some people. They also cause unsteadiness (inability to walk a straight line) and poor balance (inability to stand still with eyes closed and head tilted back).

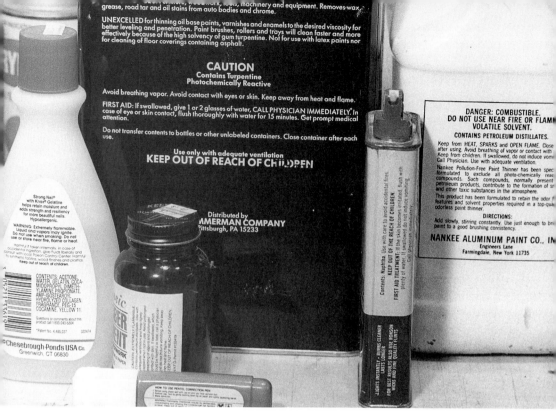

Most products containing solvents carry labels warning of the dangers of misuse.

Many solvents irritate the nervous system. This irritation causes tremors (shaky hands) and convulsions. Sensations of tightness in the chest and difficulty in breathing are also common.

How Are Solvents Absorbed?
Solvents are absorbed through the mucus linings of the throat and lungs. They are absorbed very rapidly. From the lungs, solvents are carried rapidly by the blood to all parts of the body. They are retained in the vital organs in high concentrations. These organs include the heart, lungs,

liver, and kidneys. Solvents are also retained in high concentrations in the
brain.

Many solvents enter through the nose
and are absorbed directly by the brain. At
the top of each nostril is a small, thin
bone about the size of a postage stamp.
This bone has nerves passing through it.
Some solvents pass directly through this
bone into the olfactory bulb, which is
responsible for the sense of smell. From
the olfactory bulb, they diffuse to other
parts of the brain.

How Are Solvents Eliminated?

The rate at which toluene leaves the body
is typical of other solvents. It takes about
12 hours for half of the toluene that is
absorbed by the body to disappear. This
is in a lean (thin) person. In a chubby
person, the toluene can linger as long as
65 hours! This puts a big strain on the
lungs, liver, and kidneys.

About 80% of the toluene that is absorbed is metabolized (broken down) in
the liver. The breakdown products are
eliminated in the urine. The remaining
20% of the toluene is exhaled (breathed
out) into the air.

16 | *Just How Dangerous Are Solvents?*

Exposure to levels of 2000 to 3250 ppm may cause death within 30 minutes. Exposure to 5000 ppm may cause death within just a few minutes.

Although its exact nature is not known, a new syndrome has been described. It is called the sudden sniffing death syndrome. It occurs when the sniffing of solvents is followed by physical or emotional stress. Death then occurs from heart failure.

Many chemical solvents damage vital organs. Carbon tetrachloride, for example, damages the liver and kidneys.

Liver damage is quite serious. You have only one liver. If you damage your liver beyond repair you will die.

Many solvents are carcinogens. That is, they cause cancer. Benzene is an example of a common solvent that can cause cancer.

Other Abused Inhalants—Aerosol Propellants

An aerosol can is a pressurized container. It holds a liquid material and a propellant. A propellant is a gas under pressure, which pushes the liquid out of the container. The aerosol can was developed

Many household items contain solvents.

18 during World War II. The first product was a bug bomb that contained DDT.

Between the end of the war and the early 1970s, a variety of aerosol products were put on the market. These included perfume, hair spray, paint, shoe polish, furniture wax, car wax, deodorant, and products to mask bad odors (air fresheners). The fresheners act by altering our sense of smell. They do not remove the offensive odor.

The propellants are fluorocarbons. They are available under a number of brand names, which include Freon, Genetron, Kaiser, Racon, Isotron. The fluorocarbons are also used in refrigerators and air conditioners.

Fluorocarbons are also depressants. They cause confusion and other physical problems. Paints, hair sprays, deodorants, and air fresheners provide a double hit. They contain a variety of solvents. The effect of two or more solvents inhaled at the same time is called a double hit.

When the fluorocarbons are sprayed into a balloon or plastic bag, they may partially liquefy. When inhaled, they can freeze the soft tissues of the throat. This can cause difficulty in breathing. In severe cases, it can cause death.

Because of environmental concerns, aerosol cans using fluorocarbon propellants are being phased out. The use of fluorocarbon in air conditioners and refrigerators is also being phased out. Other chemicals are being introduced for the purpose. It is not clear what will happen to people who inhale these chemicals. The toxicity of these replacements is also not known.

Volatile Anesthetic—Nitrous Oxide

Ether is another solvent that people have used for sniffing. Observing that people became unconscious after sniffing ether led physicians to the use of ether as an anesthetic. The first report of the recreational use of ether appeared in the 1700s! So sniffing is not a new problem.

The volatile (gaseous) anesthetics, ether and chloroform, were first used in midwifery (obstetrics) and surgery in the 1840s and 1850s. Neither chloroform nor ether is used in anesthesia today. Both are extremely flammable. They cause a variety of problems, including excessive bleeding.

Ether and chloroform are less prevalent than solvents and aerosols, but they are sometimes used as cleaning fluids

Storekeepers who carry possible inhalants keep an eye out
for potential abusers.

or lighter fluids. Another anesthetic, nitrous oxide, is more readily available to sniffers.

Nitrous oxide is used as the propellant in aerosol containers of whipped cream. In order to expel the whipped cream, the container is held upside down. The nitrous oxide, under pressure, forces the whipped cream out of the container. Sniffers hold the container upright. The nitrous oxide is released without the whipped cream.

Nitrites—Another Form of Inhalant Abuse

Nitrites are classified as inhalants. Amyl nitrite (Aspirol, Vaporole) is supplied in small glass capsules. It is used to treat angina pectoris (chest pain). Angina occurs when the blood vessels that lead to the heart are constricted and cannot supply enough blood. Amyl nitrite dilates the blood vessels so that more blood can reach the heart.

Amyl nitrite is a prescription drug, but it is available on the street. It does not cause intoxication. It decreases social and sexual inhibitions. It reportedly increases sexual arousal and prolongs the sensation of orgasm.

22   Butyl nitrite is chemically a close relative of amyl nitrite. It is not listed as a controlled substance by the F.D.A. (Food and Drug Administration). It has the same effects as amyl nitrite.

How Common Is Inhalant Abuse?
The National Institute of Drug Abuse (NIDA) found that at least 15% of all children asked have admitted to having used inhalants at least once. Boys and girls as young as six have experimented with solvents. One in five kids has tried using inhalants by the time of reaching the fifth grade.

About 3% become habitual users. It is believed that from 2 to 10% of habitual users use inhalants every day. Most sniffers use inhalants from several times a week to three or four times a month.

Nitrite abusers tend to be looking for different effects from the other inhalant abusers. They also tend to start abuse at an older age (25 years, as opposed to 13 years for other inhalant abusers).

CHAPTER 2

How Does It All Begin?

Jack began abusing inhalants when he was in the third grade. He got them from his neighborhood hobby shop. The store kept the model airplane glue locked up in a wire cage. Jack, who was small for his age, was able to reach into the cage.

Carl, his brother, had talked Jack into stealing glue.

To distract the storekeeper, Carl and his friends made small purchases in another part of the store.

Carl squeezed a couple of containers of glue out into a paper bag. He was the leader of the gang, so he sniffed first from the bag. He passed the bag on to Darren, who did the same thing.

24   They would continue to pass the bag around until each guy was drunk. Sometimes they let Jack take a hit as well.

Jack did not really like the smell of the glue. It made him feel sick to his stomach. He also felt lightheaded.

But hanging around with Carl and his gang members made Jack feel important. Especially when his own friends noticed.

Soon, Jack was telling his friends how to sniff glue. It made him feel as if he were the head of his own gang.

Jack is now 25. He has never held a steady job or had a steady girlfriend. He has been in trouble with the law several times. He has been caught shoplifting.

Spray Paint: A Double Hit

Phil does inhalants several times a week. His favorite is metallic spray paint, when he can get it. It gives him a double hit because it contains a higher concentration of solvents than any other spray paint. He gets the effect of the propellant Freon, as well as of the solvent toluene.

But it is getting harder for Phil to steal paint. Most auto parts stores in his neighborhood have begun to lock up the spray paints. The department stores in

Many people are not aware of the potential dangers
of solvents.

the malls have begun to do the same
thing.

Even when he has money, Phil has a
problem buying spray paint. Store owners
are unwilling to sell too many cans to the
same person.

Liquid Paper

When Phil cannot get spray paint, he
settles for liquid paper. He likes the thinner in the little jars of liquid paper. He
can get it virtually anywhere, and the
small jars are easy to conceal.

Two or three containers of thinner or
white-out will keep him high for a whole day.

A drug counselor told Phil that liquid

26 paper thinner was a chemical called 1,1,1-trichlorethane. The counselor told Phil that this chemical was more toxic than carbon tetrachloride.

These chemicals cause damage to the liver and kidneys. They can cause cirrhosis of the liver. Drinking alcohol while using one of these chemicals increases the negative effects. Calcium deficiency caused by poor diet also increases the negative effects. These chemicals can cause permanent brain damage.

The counselor also told Phil that liquid paper thinner can cause a heart attack. But Phil did not believe him. He believed that he was so young and strong, nothing could hurt him.

Phil had been drinking and sniffing paint. One night, while asleep, he vomited and sucked the vomit into his lungs. He died without ever awakening, three weeks before his 23rd birthday.

Nitrous Oxide

Miguel started abusing inhalants when he was in college. He noticed that a couple of his friends were buying a lot of whipped cream topping cartridges and taking them to their room to do whip-its.

Miguel was curious and asked them what was going on. They told him that the propellant for whipped cream was nitrous oxide.

They invited Miguel to join them. They showed him how to release the gas. Just a couple of cartridges were enough to get Miguel high.

Miguel liked using it. It had very little taste or smell. He never had the smell of alcohol on his breath. He never got a hangover.

He found that nitrous oxide decreased his inhibitions. He could talk to girls without feeling embarrassed or insecure.

Miguel did some reading about nitrous oxide. He found out it was first made by Joseph Priestley in 1776.

By the early 1800s, nitrous oxide parties were fashionable. "Turned on" became an expression in use.

Miguel thought that nitrous oxide was safe. But, to make sure, he asked a friend who was in medical school. His friend told Miguel that the prolonged use of nitrous oxide could damage bone marrow. Bone marrow is where the blood cells are made. Nitrous oxide can also damage the brain.

Miguel decided to stop using nitrous

Teens who don't use drugs face the pressure of their peers to try them.

oxide. He tried to tell his friends these facts, but they did not seem to care. They continued to use nitrous oxide often.

No-Stick Coating (Freon)

It was the middle of summer. Mindy and Cissy were bored. They were both 13. They decided to try to get high. They had watched a TV talk show about inhalants.

They decided to try no-stick frying pan coating. Mindy sniffed first, then Cissy tried it. She liked it so much she did it again.

Then Cissy got a funny look on her face. She became hysterical and ran rapidly around the room. She screamed and waved her arms. She ran out into the backyard, then back into the living room. Then she collapsed!

Mindy was really frightened. She called 911 and the ambulance arrived in four minutes. The paramedics worked on Cissy for several minutes. Then they took her to the hospital.

Cissy was dead by the time they got to the hospital!

Mindy called her parents. She told them what she and Cissy had done. Her

30 | parents called Cissy's mom. They had to break the news about what had happened.

Cissy's mom arrived at the hospital. The doctor told her that Cissy had died sniffing propellants. She died of sudden sniffing death syndrome.

There were three chemical substances in the aerosol container. One was lecithin. It is what makes the no-stick surface. The can also held trichloromonofluoromethane and dichlordifluoromethane, which are propellants. They are commonly referred to as Freon, which is a trade name. Genetron and Isotron are other trade names.

The doctor explained that high concentrations of Freon may increase the sensitivity of the heart to several hormones that are normally present in the body. Those hormones are adrenalin and noradrenalin.

These two hormones cause an increase in the heart rate. In the presence of Freon, they can cause the heart to beat so fast that the person develops arrhythmia. This is an abnormal beating rhythm—generally too fast.

Cissy died because her heart developed arrhythmia.

CHAPTER 3

What Else Do People Use?

*J*oe lived in a rural area. He was in second grade when he and his three friends decided to get high.

Gasoline

They siphoned some gasoline from Joe's dad's pickup and inhaled it to get high. Joe went first, then passed the plastic bag on to Ramon. He passed the bag on to Les. Les likes to show off so he took ten deep breaths. Les could not stand up. He tried to pass the bag to Manny, but Manny did not want to try it. He left.

So Les passed the bag back to Joe, who took seven or eight deep breaths. Joe and his friends could keep a bag going for

Leading a busy, satisfying life helps teens to stay drug-free.

three to four hours. By that time, they would be very drunk.

Joe and his family moved into town when he started fourth grade. Joe did not like his new school. He felt insecure, and the kids made fun of him. He did not fit in and didn't have any friends.

Lighter Fluid

It was hard for Joe to get gasoline. Someone always seemed to be around.

Then he discovered lighter fluid. Someone told him it was butane. He

didn't care if it was dangerous or not. He 33
could get it from disposable lighters and
could stay high all day.

He only went to school once or twice a
week. The rest of the time he got high.
His mom didn't seem to notice. She was
busy with the other kids, and she went
out to work. When he was high, he didn't
care what anyone said or did.

When Joe was in seventh grade, the
man in the store down the street caught
him stealing lighters and called the police.
The police took him in.

They called his mom at work. She
had to take time off to pick him up at
the police station and was really upset.
She said, "I could lose my job! Then
what would we do? Where would we
go?"

His mom made Joe promise that he
would not steal lighters any more. He
also had to promise to go to school every
day and to go to the community center
after school.

Joe was scared. He did go to school
every day for a couple of weeks. He was
afraid to go back to stealing lighters. He
felt miserable and he needed to get high.
Soon! He didn't want to go back to the
same stores again.

34 | *Charcoal Starter (Petroleum Ether)*

Joe took the bus to the supermarket about two miles from his house. He wandered up and down the aisles. Finally, he saw something called charcoal starter. He stole a can.

He found a culvert down the street from the store and crawled in. Soon he was flying high.

All of a sudden, he noticed two or three big guys at each end of the culvert. They were watching him. One of the guys asked him what he was doing.

Joe said that he was using charcoal starter to get high. The big guys moved into the culvert. They said they wanted to try it, so Joe showed them how.

When he was 16, Joe's mother kicked him out of the house. He dropped out of school. Now he lives on the street and gets high whenever he can.

Nail Polish Remover (Acetone)

Leta is 14. She discovered something while she was doing her nails. The nail polish remover made her feel woozy and she liked the feeling.

Leta is really shy. She doesn't have any friends. She's also jealous of the other girls at school because they are beginning

Products containing solvents are useful when used properly.

36 to develop adult bodies. Leta thinks she looks like a guy.

Leta became an expert at sniffing acetone nail polish remover. Leta could go into the bathroom at school and take a few sniffs anytime. After a few sniffs, she would not feel shy anymore. She could talk to the kids at school. And they talked to her.

After a few weeks, her mom wanted to know what she was doing with all the nail polish and remover.

Leta became desperate. If she could not get high, she was afraid she would not be able to talk to the other kids.

Hair Spray (Freon)

So she tried other things. Soon, Leta discovered that she could get high on hair spray. She could get little cans that she could carry in her purse. She could sniff it anytime she felt insecure.

She found the kind that worked best had Freon and polyvinylpyrrolidone.

When she was a junior, Leta got really sick. She nearly died. She damaged her liver and had to stay in the hospital for more than a month.

Since then, Leta has been afraid of getting high. She has been talking to a

Aerosol sprays are harmful for both your health and
the environment.

counselor at school who is helping her to overcome being shy.

Paint Thinner (Propyl)

Gilly started sniffing paint thinner when he was 13. Sniffing made him feel dizzy. Being dizzy made him feel sick.

Gilly does not like being high, but all his friends do it. If he does not sniff, his friends call him chicken.

Many of the kids in Gilly's school do worse things. Heroin, crack, or whatever! Things that are illegal. If you are caught with drugs, you could go to jail.

Gilly's friends steal paint thinner, glue, nail polish remover—anything to get high. They think Gilly steals, but he actually buys his paint thinner. His older brother went to jail for stealing.

Most of Gilly's friends get mean when they get high. They once beat up a guy from another school.

Gilly has started to fake getting high. He pours a small amount of paint thinner onto his rag and does not take deep breaths.

At 15, Gilly has dropped out of school. He has found a job flipping hamburgers. He has stopped getting high. He plans to get his GED (General Education Diploma). He has saved himself.

CHAPTER 4

When Does It Begin?

Jerry is 15. His mother and grandmother call him Gerardo, but he does not like that name. That is his father's name. His father left them just after Jerry was born, and they have not seen him since.

Jerry and his friends began sniffing cleaning fluids two years ago. Alonso's dad owns a dry cleaning shop. He makes Al work in the shop. So Al takes the cleaning fluid, called trichlorothane, from his father's store.

Al's dad told him that trichlorothane is dangerous.

Jerry and Al and three or four other guys get together in an abandoned building in their neighborhood. They sniff cleaning fluid a couple of times a week.

40   Al always talks about how careful his father is not to breathe the fumes. His dad is always telling him about a friend who died of a heart attack.

Jerry, Al, and the other guys think it is exciting to do something that is dangerous. Each of the guys tries to appear braver than the others.

They have gotten into more fights. They lost the last fight, and Jerry ended up with two broken ribs. They had tried to push around one of the street people in the neighborhood. He was tougher than he looked and fought back.

Within a couple of weeks, Jerry got into another fight. When he is high, he feels as if he can do anything.

One weekend, Jerry was sick. He could not go out. Al and the other guys got high. They stole a car and went joy riding.

The newspaper report says they hit an overpass pillar going 80 miles an hour. Two of the guys died instantly. Al is in a coma, and he may never wake up.

Typical Sniffers

Jerry and Al are fairly typical sniffers. They usually begin sniffing when they are around 13. Sniffing is usually done once or twice a week in groups.

Sniffing or huffing inhalants can increase violent behavior.

42   Most people stop sniffing within a few years. Unfortunately, they generally switch to another drug. Often that drug is alcohol.

Inhalants and the Brain

Inhalants are depressants. They tend to decrease activity in the cortex of the brain.

The cortex is the outer layer of the brain. It is only about a quarter of an inch thick. It contains about 70 to 80 percent of all the nerve cells in the brain.

The cortex is the part of the brain that is responsible for the traits that make humans human—things like reasoning, judgment, speech. The cortex also controls the more primitive parts of the brain.

Most of the effects of inhalants are caused by depression of the cortex. These effects are slurred speech, lack of coordination, unsteadiness, decreased inhibitions, and an increase in aggressiveness.

Inhalants impair judgment. Many users are hurt or killed in accidents, especially accidents that involve driving a car or a motorbike.

Somewhere between a third and a half of all the people who abuse inhalants

Avoiding people who do drugs makes it easier to avoid doing drugs yourself.

44 experience hallucinations. Usually the hallucinations are unpleasant or frightening.

Many users are also hurt in fights. Depressing the activity of the cortex makes them feel invincible. Nobody is invincible.

Kurt

Kurt and his friends were 15 when they decided they needed some excitement. It was the middle of the summer and there was nothing to do.

Ray told them about sniffing fire extinguishers. He learned about it at juvenile hall when he was there for shoplifting.

The other guys did not believe Ray, so he went to the hardware store and stole a fire extinguisher. Then he showed them how to use it.

Craig and Sol did not want to try it. They said it was stupid. After some pushing, shoving, and name-calling, Craig and Sol left.

The other boys passed the plastic bag around and got high. They did it for a couple of hours. By then everyone was thoroughly smashed.

They got together several more times and sniffed. Each time fewer of the guys showed up. By the middle of the summer, it was only Kurt and Ray. When Ray was

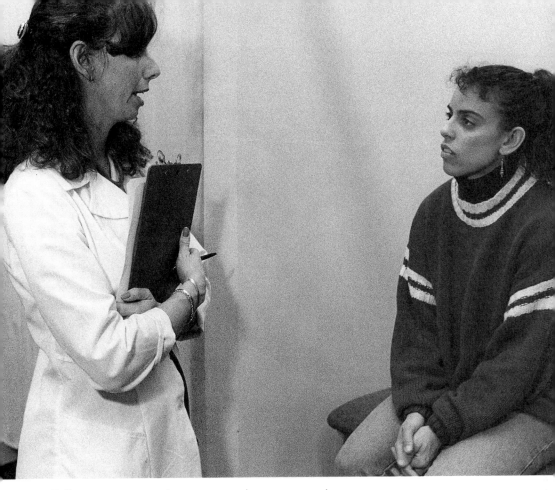

Talk to someone such as a counselor or nurse who can accurately answer your questions about drugs or drug use.

arrested for stealing a car, Kurt stopped sniffing.

Kurt and the guys drink beer when they can get it. Kurt visited Ray a couple of times. Ray still sniffs fire extinguishers when he can. He has joined another gang.

Toward the end of the summer, Kurt heard that Craig had found a job at the supermarket. He wants to save money to buy a car. He is trying to get Sol a job there, too.

CHAPTER 5

Where Can You Go for Help?

*R*ick was 14. He and some of his friends thought it might be fun to get high. They had tried it once before, when Sammy had stolen a fifth of tequila from a liquor store.

They had passed the bottle around. Soon everyone was acting really funny and they could hardly talk or stand up. The tequila had a strong taste. It was hard to drink it straight.

Model Airplane Glue (Toluene)

They wanted to try something new. One of the guys said that his big brother sometimes sniffed airplane glue and that maybe they should try that.

Each of the guys went to one of the stores in the neighborhood and bought several tubes of glue.

They waited till Saturday and got together in the shack they used as a hangout. They opened several of the tubes of glue, took out a plastic bag, and began the process of sniffing.

A bag lasted about three hours, until the sides got stuck together. Then they started a new bag, with fresh glue.

Two or three of the guys got together several times a week. They got high on the glue. When the glue ran out, Rick wanted to get more. But the other guys were not interested.

Spray Paint (Freon and Toluene)

Rick continued to use glue whenever he could get it, but it became harder and harder to get. Then he discovered metallic spray paint. At first he bought the paint, but it was more expensive than glue. So he began to steal it.

Rick's parents worked hard. His mom worked in an office and his dad had two jobs. Rick was home alone a lot.

Rick's parents noticed that his grades began to slip. He had been a B student, but now he was getting Ds and Fs.

You may experience withdrawal symptoms when you stop doing drugs.

They also noticed that his nose and eyes were red and runny. His breath smelled terrible. He did not eat much. Sometimes he appeared dazed or dizzy.

49

His mother saw that he had an odd-looking rash. It was a reddened area around his nose and mouth, in the shape of a triangle.

Getting Help

Rick's parents were worried about him. Rick claimed he felt fine and did not have any problems. But they decided to take him to Dr. MacIntosh.

Dr. Mac took one look at Rick and knew what his problem was. He asked to speak to Rick alone.

When Rick's parents left, Dr. Mac asked if he was sniffing something like typewriter correction fluid, gasoline, model airplane glue, paint, or anything else. At first Rick lied and said he was not sniffing anything.

The doctor kept pressing. Finally, Rick admitted that he was sniffing paint. He told Dr. Mac that he had been doing it for about nine months.

Dr. Mac called Rick's parents into the room. He said that Rick had a problem.

50 He was abusing inhalants. He was sniffing metallic spray paint.

He said he would try to help Rick, but he would need their help and the help of professionals.

Propellants and Solvents

Rick was actually abusing two kinds of inhalants. The first kind was the propellant. This is the chemical that "pushes" the paint out of the can.

The second was the solvents. The paint was dissolved in the solvents. Metallic paint requires more solvents than any other types of spray paint.

The propellant was probably Freon or propane. Either one could make you drunk.

The combination solvent was probably a mixture of benzene, toluene, xylene, and other chemicals. They can all cause intoxication.

Tolerance

The body can get used to the presence of a drug. The effect of a given amount is reduced. So the person must take a larger dose to achieve the same effect. People can build up a tolerance for drugs like alcohol, heroin, or cocaine.

There is evidence that many solvents can cause a tolerance to build up. Some propellants may do the same. Tolerance is one component of dependence.

51

Withdrawal

Dr. Mac explained that after tolerance, the second component of dependence is withdrawal. He said Rick would experience some unpleasant feelings when he stopped abusing spray paint. He would probably experience some hand tremors (shaking). Chronic headaches and nervousness are also common. He might also sweat a lot.

The doctor said it was thought unlikely that these solvents or propellants cause physical dependence. But they do cause an intense psychological craving for the effects of the chemicals.

Tests

Dr. Mac ran some tests on Rick. He checked his liver, kidneys, lungs, and heart. He also checked Rick's blood to be sure Rick was not anemic.

Dr. Mac made an appointment for Rick to see a psychoneurologist. That is a doctor who performs a variety of

52 | psychological tests to determine if there are any changes in intelligence. He also gives tests of memory, attention, and concentration.

Counseling

Dr. Mac also recommended counseling for Rick to help with his psychological dependence.

Counselors often work with people on a one-on-one basis. They also work with groups of people with similar problems. Dr. Mac explained about the various kinds of therapists and counselors.

Psychologists and social workers treat people who have problems. They use behavioral methods for treating these disorders. They cannot prescribe drugs as part of the treatment.

Psychiatrists, on the other hand, are medical doctors. They specialize in the treatment of people with mental problems. They can prescribe drugs as part of the treatment.

Psychiatrists, psychologists, and social workers must be licensed to practice. To be licensed, they must have a certain level of training and professional experience. In some states, counselors do not need to be licensed.

Unfortunately, a license does not guar- |
antee that a counselor or therapist is competent or ethical. The best way to choose one of these professionals is to get a recommendation from someone you know well and trust. Family doctors or school counselors are a good source of information.

Dr. Mac recommended Dr. Dillard, a psychiatrist who has a large practice and several psychologists and social workers working for him.

Dr. Dillard told Rick and his parents that it was hard to know how long the treatment would take. It would depend on how Rick reacted to therapy.

Dr. Dillard explained that he or one of his associates would see Rick several times each week for several weeks to help Rick deal with his psychological dependence.

They would also try to determine why he turned to inhalants in the first place. After a few weeks, they would start Rick in group therapy.

Group Therapy

These groups are made up of people with similar problems. A professional meets with each group once a week. He or she

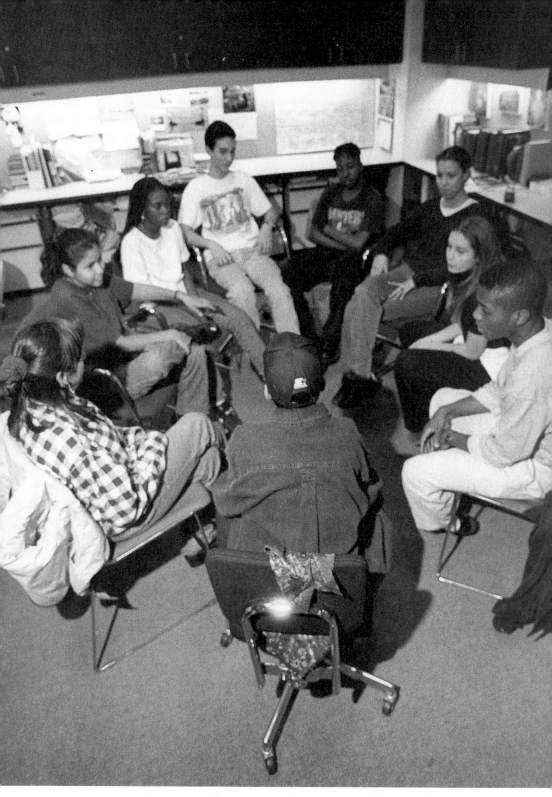
Peer counseling groups offer support and help in dealing with life's challenges.

acts as a facilitator to keep the discussion | *55*
on target.

Group therapy will help Rick identify the stresses in his life and learn how to deal with them.

It will also help him develop better social skills.

Dr. Dillard said it was important for Rick's parents to come to some of the sessions. It is vital to keep the lines of communication open.

Self-Help Groups

Self-help groups are made up of people with the same type of problem. They usually meet weekly or biweekly. They discuss their problems and try to help each other.

Self-help groups modeled after Alcoholics Anonymous seem to be especially successful in dealing with problems of chemical abuse. The original 12 steps provide a philosophy and principles for dealing with problems.

Support Groups

Support groups are for the family and friends of a person with a chemical abuse problem. They provide emotional support and help in coping with the problems associated with substance abuse.

Support groups can give you the strength you need to maintain your health and independence.

These groups are usually not run by a therapist. Many groups invite speakers. Some just get together to talk and share ideas. They are usually free.

Fact Sheet

- Inhalant use by high school seniors has increased steadily at a time when most other drug use has declined, according to the NIDA.
- Five to 15 percent of young children have experimented with inhalants.
- About half of all young people who try inhalants show signs of continuing abuse.
- First use of inhalants precedes the use of other drugs, including tobacco, alcohol, marijuana, and amphetamines.
- A survey of New York State high school students found that 10.6% had used inhalants in the previous six months.
- According to the same survey, 33% of those receiving failing grades were inhalant users.
- Chronic users of inhalants use them because they are low in cost, easily available, have convenient packaging, and cause rapid intoxication. These products are normally sold over the counter. They are drugs.
- More than 5 million people use nitrites at least once a week, according to the NIDA survey.
- Inhalant abuse is believed to lead to dangerous driving, property damage, shoplifting, and theft.

Glossary
Explaining New Words

addiction Intense physiological and psychological craving for a drug.

aerosol Gas that is used to propel (push) other substances out of a pressurized can.

anesthetics Gases and drugs that are used to cause unconsciousness and numbness to pain.

carcinogen Substance that causes cancer.

depressant Substance that decreases the activity of the nervous system.

Freon Brand name of a common aerosol propellant and refrigerant.

inhalant Chemical that is volatile and gives off fumes.

intoxicant Drug or chemical that causes the user to feel and act drunk.

invincible Incapable of being conquered.

nitrite Drug used to cause dilation of blood vessels.

nitrous oxide   Anesthetic commonly
 used in dentistry and for minor surgery. Also the propellant for whipped
 topping, such as whipped cream.

obstetrics   The science of assisting
 women during pregnancy and at
 childbirth.

solvent   Volatile substance, in which
 things dissolve.

tolerance   Ability to resist the effect of
 a drug.

toluene   Solvent.

volatile   Capable of changing from a
 liquid to a gas at room temperature.

withdrawal   Physical symptoms that
 occur when a drug is withheld from a
 person addicted to it.

Help List

Associations
The National Institute of Drug Abuse (NIDA)
1-800-662-HELP
Monday–Friday 9 a.m. to 8 p.m.

National Association of Alcoholism and Drug Abuse Counselors
3717 Columbia Pike
Arlington, VA 22204
1-713-920-4644

National Clearinghouse for Alcohol and Drug Information
P.O. Box 2345
Rockville, MD 20852
1-301-468-2600

Support Groups
Narcotics Anonymous
P.O. Box 9999
Van Nuys, CA 91409
1-818-780-3951

Families Anonymous
P.O. Box 538
Van Nuys, CA 91408
1-818-989-7941

Toughlove   *61*
P.O. Box 1069
Doylestown, PA 18901
1-800-33-1069

In Canada
**Alcohol and Drug Dependency Informa-
  tion and Counseling Services
  (ADDICS)**
#2, 2471½ Portage Avenue
Winnepeg, MB R3J 0N6
204-831-1999

Narcotics Anonymous
P.O. Box 7500, Station A
Toronto, ON M5W 1P9
416-691-9519

For Further Reading

Ball, Jacqueline A. *Everything You Need to Know About Drug Abuse.* New York: Rosen Publishing Group, Inc., 1994, rev. ed.

Hurwitz, Sue, and Shniderman, Nancy. *Drugs and Your Friends.* New York: Rosen Publishing Group, 1993.

McKay, Matthew, and Fanning, Patrick. *Self-Esteem.* Oakland, CA: New Harbinger, 1987.

Rawls, Bea O'Donnell, and Johnson, Gwen. *Drugs and Where to Turn.* New York: Rosen Publishing Group, 1993.

Watson, Joyce M. *Solvent Abuse: The Adolescent Epidemic?* London: Croom Helm, 1986.

Yoder, Barbara. *The Recovery Resource Book.* New York: Fireside (Simon & Schuster), 1990.

Index

About the Author
Dr. Clifford Sherry is a senior scientist and principal investigator with Systems Research Laboratories. He has taught human physiology and psychopharmacology to more than 2,000 students. He has professional publications in more than 30 scientific journals. He has written three books, including *Drugs and Eating Disorders*.

Photo Credits
Cover photo by Maje Waldo; all other photos by Lauren Piperno.